ATTAINMENT'S
Right On Reader 2

Pamela J. Mims • Angel Lee • Tracie-Lynn Zakas • Diane M. Browder

Right On Reader 2

Pamela J. Mims
Angel Lee
Tracie-Lynn Zakas
Diane M. Browder

Graphic design: Elizabeth Ragsdale & Sherry Pribbenow
Illustration: Jo Reynolds & Beverly Sanders
Editing: Linda R. Schreiber

An Attainment Company Publication
©2013 Attainment Company, Inc. All rights reserved.
Printed in the United States of America
ISBN: 1-57861-959-9

Attainment Company, Inc.
P.O. Box 930160 • Verona, Wisconsin 53593-0160 USA
Phone: 800-327-4269 • Fax: 800.942.3865
www.AttainmentCompany.com

Contents

UNIT THREE

Number the Stars 7

The Diary of Anne Frank . . . 73

When You Turn Out
     the Light. 83

UNIT FOUR

Dragonwings 89

Sadako and the Thousand
      Paper Cranes 157

One Tribe 175

UNIT THREE
Social Justice

Number the Stars

By Lois Lowry

Based on the book *Number the Stars,* by Lois Lowry.

7

CHAPTER

1 Life in Copenhagen 9

2 Changes in Denmark 15

3 Trouble for Jewish People 22

4 Good Weather for Fishing 30

5 A Need for Courage 36

6 Unwelcome Visitors 43

7 Annemarie Helps Out 50

8 The Important Package 57

9 The Handkerchief Saves People 62

10 Ellen's Necklace 68

CHAPTER 1

Life in Copenhagen

Annemarie, her younger sister, Kirsti, and her best friend,    Ellen Rosen, lived in Copenhagen, Denmark. One day they    were running home from school when they were stopped by two German soldiers. The Germans had been in Denmark for three years at the time. The soldiers were Nazis and they were bad people. The soldiers asked the girls questions.   They wanted to know why the girls were running.

The girls got stopped by German soldiers.

Annemarie told them it was because they had races every    Friday at school. One soldier asked Annemarie what was in her backpack. She told him she had school books. The soldiers then let the girls go. They told them not to run because it made them look like hoodlums. The girls walked home as quickly  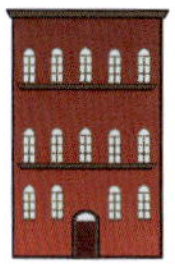 and quietly as possible. When they got to the building    where their families lived, they walked in quietly. That kept the soldiers, who were standing there, from noticing them.

The girls got stopped by German soldiers.

Ellen said she was scared, and Annemarie said she was too.   They did not want to tell their mothers what happened.

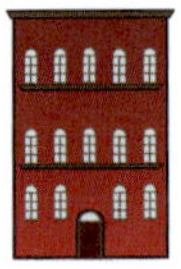

They went into their own apartments. Annemarie's mother,    Mrs. Johansen, and Ellen's mother, Mrs. Rosen, were having     coffee in Annemarie's apartment. When Kirsti got to the door, she decided to tell her mother what happened. Both mothers    were worried. Mrs. Johansen and Mrs. Rosen talked about how 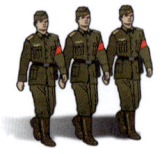    the soldiers stopping people on the street made them worried. Annemarie pretended she was not listening to the mothers

talking. She heard her mother whisper that their friend, Peter, brought them a newspaper they were not supposed to have. 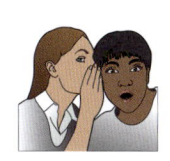    They whispered that they wanted the girls to walk to school a different way. Then, Mrs. Rosen left to go talk to her daughter. The girls were hungry but there was not much food to eat.  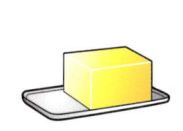   They ate bread with no butter. Kirsti wanted a cupcake. Her    mother explained there was no sugar to make cupcakes. The

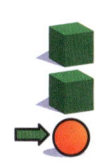

soldiers took the sugar. There would be no sugar until the war ended and the soldiers left.

The girls got stopped by German soldiers.

CHAPTER 2

Changes in Denmark

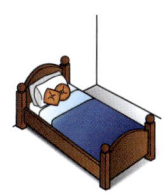

Annemarie and Kirsti went to bed. Kirsti wanted to hear a story about kings and queens. Annemarie started to tell the story, but Kirsti fell fast asleep. Annemarie thought about the real king of Denmark, called King Christian X. He was different from fairy tale kings. People in Denmark loved him.

Everyone protected the king.

One day, a  Nazi soldier saw  King Christian X riding his  horse on the  street. The  soldier asked who the man was. When the  soldier heard it was the  king, he asked who was  protecting the  king. The man  answered that everyone in  Denmark  protected the  king.  Annemarie asked her  father why the  king could not  protect them from the  Nazis. Her  father said because  Denmark was a small country and King Christian X knew Denmark could    not win against the Nazis. Instead, the king chose to protect his people by not fighting. Annemarie told her father that Nazis were not in Sweden. Her father said she was right. Sweden was still a free country. She remembered seeing Sweden across the ocean from her Uncle Henrik's house. Annemarie thought about all the changes since her father told her that story. It had

3

been almost three years. Sweden was still free. King Christian X

was still alive.

Everyone protected the king.

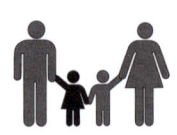

At one time, Annemarie had an older sister, Lise. Thinking of

Lise made Annemarie sad. Lise died several years earlier in an

2

accident. She died just two weeks before she was supposed

to marry Peter. There was a blue trunk in Annemarie's room.

It was filled with things for Lise and  Peter and their  wedding. Annemarie's  mother and  father never  talked about Lise. They all still  loved Peter very much.  Peter did not  marry anyone else after Lise  died. When  Peter came to the  apartment, he  talked to Mr. and  Mrs. Johansen about things  Annemarie did not  understand. Happily, the  girls did not have any more  trouble with the  soldiers. Their  mothers started to prepare for the hard

winter ahead. Annemarie shared a bed with her sister. That    helped them both stay warm. One day, Mrs. Johansen saw that    Kirsti's jacket was missing a button. She sent the girls to a sewing shop to get a new one. When they got there, the     shop was closed. Mrs. Johansen was upset when Annemarie told her the shop was closed. She went to talk to Mrs. Rosen. That night when Annemarie was in bed, her mother came to get

her. Peter Neilsen had come to visit. He brought them gifts.    Annemarie was happy, but knew it was dangerous for him to    be there. Mr. Johansen said the German soldiers closed shops owned by Jews. Annemarie remembered the Rosens were Jewish.     Mr. Rosen was a teacher, not a shop owner. After Peter visited for a while, he left and Annemarie went back to bed.

Everyone protected the king.

CHAPTER 3

Trouble for Jewish People

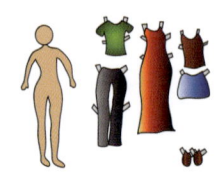

Ellen and Annemarie liked to play with paper dolls. One day,     Mrs. Johansen and Kirsti came home from shoe shopping. Kirsti was upset that the store did not have shoes made of leather.    There was no leather because of the war. Annemarie let Kirsti play with some of their paper dolls. They pretended to go see

gardens in Copenhagen. Kirsti talked about the fireworks they saw on her birthday. The fireworks were in the garden. This    reminded Annemarie of the time when the Danish people blew  up their own ships. They did this to keep the Germans from   using them. When it happened, Mrs. Johansen told Kirsti the    explosions were fireworks for her birthday. Annemarie did not want to play anymore. Ellen went home to help her mother

set up for the Jewish New Year. She invited Annemarie and     Kirsti to come on Thursday night to watch her mother light   the candles. On Thursday afternoon, Mrs. Rosen came by and 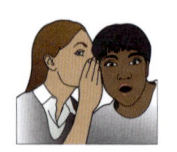   whispered something to Mrs. Johansen. Then she left. Mrs.    Johansen told the girls that Ellen was going to stay with them.

Ellen wore a necklace.

That night, Ellen's parents went to visit some family members

out of town. Once Kirsti went to bed, Mr. Johansen told    Annemarie what really happened. The Nazis had a list of   local Jews, and they were coming to their houses to take     them away. Peter took Ellen's parents to a safe place to hide from the Nazis. Annemarie's family kept Ellen with them. They pretended she was part of the family. Annemarie and Ellen got ready to go to bed. Annemarie saw a Star of David necklace

around Ellen's neck. Ellen asked Annemarie if the soldiers would search the apartment. Annemarie did not think so. Ellen said that if the soldiers came, she would pretend to be Lise. Ellen asked how Lise died, but Annemarie did not know. Lise and     Peter were out together, and Annemarie's parents were told there was an accident. Her parents went to the hospital to see Lise, but she had already died.

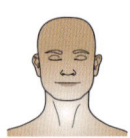

Ellen wore a necklace.

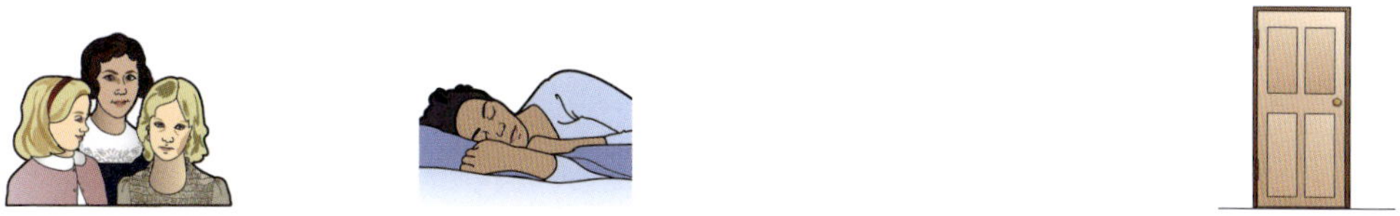

After the girls went to sleep, a pounding on the door of the apartment woke them up. A soldier asked Annemarie's father where the Rosens were. Mrs. Johansen said they must be asleep in their apartment. The soldiers came in to look for them.

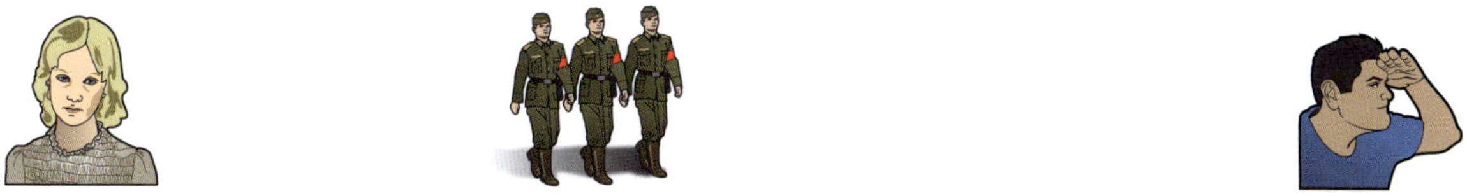

Annemarie heard the soldiers. She knew that if they saw the Star of David necklace, they would know Ellen was Jewish.

Annemarie pulled the necklace off of Ellen just as the soldiers came into her room. The soldiers made the girls get up. They asked them lots of questions. The soldiers wanted to know why two of the girls had blonde hair, while the other had dark hair. Mr. Johansen grabbed a picture of his three girls. Two of the girls in the picture had blonde hair, and one had dark hair. Lise had dark hair. Annemarie held the Star of David necklace the whole time the soldiers were there.

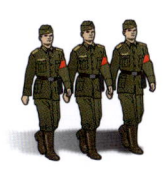

Ellen wore a necklace.

CHAPTER 4

Good Weather for Fishing

Mr. and Mrs. Johansen thought about what to do. Ellen    was sorry her dark hair caused trouble for the Johansens. Mrs. Johansen told Ellen they were lucky Lise had dark hair in her baby picture. The Johansens decided that Ellen and Annemarie would go to Uncle Henrik's house instead of school. Mrs.

Johansen said she would take them. Mr.  Johansen called  Henrik and asked if the  weather was good for  fishing.

The girls  visited Uncle  Henrik.

Mr.  Johansen said his  wife was coming to  visit and bringing a  package.  Annemarie realized her  father was  talking in code. She knew the  package meant  Ellen. Mr. Johansen told  Henrik that other  packages would come soon. Mrs.  Johansen,  Annemarie,

Kirsti, and Ellen took the train to Uncle Henrik's house. While they were on the train, soldiers went through their car. They asked Mrs. Johansen if she was going to visit someone for the New Year. Annemarie knew the New Year was a Jewish holiday, and that the soldiers wanted to know if they were Jewish. Annemarie was afraid Kirsti would say it was Ellen's New Year. But Kirsti didn't say anything to the soldiers, and they left.

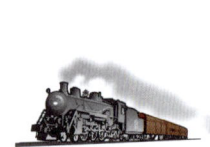

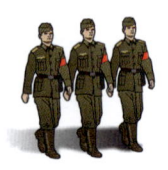

After they got off the train, they walked to the house where Mrs. Johansen had grown up and where Uncle Henrik now lived.

The girls visited Uncle Henrik.

When they got there, Ellen said it was the first time she    had seen the ocean. Annemarie looked for her uncle's boat.    She could not see it, but she could see Sweden. Uncle Henrik's house was in Denmark, but it was close to Sweden. You could see Sweden across the ocean. The girls entered Henrik's house. Mrs. Johansen told them not to speak to anyone. The girls    asked Mrs. Johansen if there were soldiers there. Mrs. Johansen said soldiers were everywhere. The girls went upstairs to bed. Ellen asked Annemarie where her Star of David necklace was.    Annemarie said it was in a safe hiding place. She told Ellen she would keep it until it was safe to wear it again.

The girls visited Uncle Henrik.

CHAPTER 5

A Need for Courage

The next morning, Annemarie woke up at Uncle Henrik's house.    She went downstairs. Mrs. Johansen showed Annemarie a pitcher of fresh milk. They had not had fresh milk in a long time  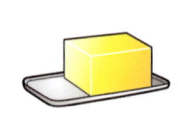  because of the war. They had butter, too. Uncle Henrik had     hidden the butter from the soldiers. Annemarie made a joke.

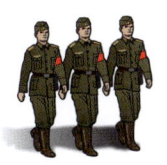

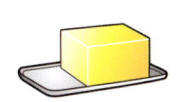

She asked if the soldiers moved butter to other places like    they did people. Mrs. Johansen laughed. The laughing helped    Annemarie feel better. The girls played outside all day.

Uncle Henrik went fishing.

Annemarie took Ellen to a small grassy pasture to see a cow.   The cow's name was Blossom. Later in the afternoon, Uncle     Henrik came home. Annemarie heard him tell her mother he would go fishing the next day. She was confused. Uncle Henrik was a fisherman. He went fishing every day. Her uncle said    they would leave the next morning and stay all night on the    boat. He asked Mrs. Johansen if they had the living room  ready. Annemarie asked why it needed to be ready. Uncle  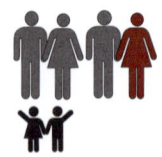  Henrik told her his aunt had died.

Uncle Henrik went fishing.

They were going to have her funeral at his house that night.  Annemarie did not understand why no one was sad, and she didn't remember having an aunt. After eating supper, Annemarie went to the barn to see Uncle Henrik. She asked him why  he lied to her. Uncle Henrik asked her how brave she was.  She told him she was not brave, but he did not believe it.  He knew Annemarie had a lot of courage. He told her it

would be easier to be brave if she did not know what was   happening. Uncle Henrik told Annemarie she did not have an 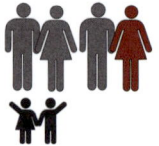   aunt. He did not tell her anything else. Some people brought a casket into Uncle Henrik's living room. Ellen told Annemarie she was sorry her aunt had died. Annemarie did not tell Ellen the truth. People began to arrive at Uncle Henrik's house. Mrs. Johansen said they were friends of her aunt. Annemarie went

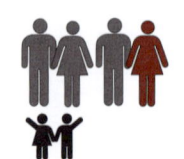

into the  kitchen to help make  food. She asked her  mother why they were making  food when usually others brought  food to  funerals. It was late and Uncle  Henrik was ready to  leave for the  boat. He  walked outside into the  darkness. When he returned,  Peter Neilsen was with him.  Ellen's  parents, the Rosens, were also there. They  hugged  Ellen tight but had  worried looks on their 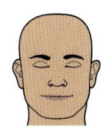 faces.

Uncle Henrik went fishing.

CHAPTER 6

Unwelcome Visitors

Uncle Henrik got ready to leave on his boat. There were people around the casket in his living room. Ellen's parents were there with Peter Neilsen and others. Ellen was sitting between her parents. Annemarie felt sad. She knew Ellen was going away.  Annemarie fell asleep in a chair. She woke up when headlights

Unit Three • Number the Stars • Chapter 6

from a car flashed into the living room. Nazi soldiers were in the car. They came to the door and pounded on it. Everyone in the room was frightened. One woman began to cry.

There was a funeral at Henrik's house.

The soldiers asked why so many people were at Uncle Henrik's house. Mrs. Johansen said a family member died. She lied to the soldiers and said her aunt had died. The soldiers did not believe her. They wanted to open the closed casket.   Mrs. Johansen said their aunt died of typhus, and if they    opened the casket, people in the room would get sick. The     soldiers believed her and left. After the soldiers left, Peter read verses from the Bible.

There was a funeral at Henrik's house.

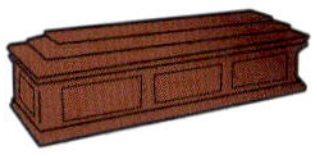

When he was done reading, he opened the casket. There was

no one in it. Instead, it was filled with blankets and clothes.

Peter gave the clothes and blankets to the people in Uncle

Henrik's living room. They would need them to stay warm.

Annemarie watched Ellen put on a jacket that was worn out.

The Rosens had pride but were not worried about wearing old

clothing. Mrs. Johansen passed out food to them. Peter gave

Mr. Rosen a paper package. He told them it was important to

give it to Henrik at the boat. Annemarie realized Mr. Rosen did not know what was in the package. He did not ask because    it was safer not to know. Peter got ready to leave but the    Rosens stayed behind. Peter told Mrs. Johansen to come in 20 minutes. Peter said good-bye to Annemarie and left. Annemarie knew that Uncle Henrik was going to take them and others to   Sweden in his boat.

Sweden was still a free country. Jews like the Rosens would be safe there. Annemarie looked one last time at the Rosens. They were sitting up straight and tall. She remembered how things were back in Copenhagen. Mr. Rosen was a teacher. Ellen liked to be in school plays. Then, she thought about how frightened they must be now. Going to Sweden across the ocean would    be dangerous because the soldiers would be looking for them.

There was a funeral at Henrik's house.

CHAPTER 7

Annemarie Helps Out

Mrs. Johansen left for the boat and the Rosens went with her.

The Rosens hugged Annemarie good-bye. Ellen and Annemarie    hugged for a long time. Ellen promised she would be back.

Annemarie sat in the living room and cried. Annemarie thought her mother should be back by 3:30 in the morning. A few

minutes later she fell asleep. The light woke Annemarie up. She looked at the clock and saw it was 4:00. Her mother should 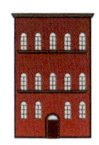   have been home already. She looked in the bedrooms but Mrs.   Johansen was not there. She went to the window thinking she   would see her returning. Instead, she saw a dark shape on the ground. It was still dark outside and, at first, Annemarie could not tell what it was. Then it moved. She saw her mother lying

on the ground. Annemarie ran out the door to her mother.

Mrs. Johansen tried to tell Annemarie she was okay.

Annemarie was brave.

She sat up but could not stand up. She was in pain.

Annemarie asked what happened. Her mother said the

Rosens were with Henrik. When she hurried to get back to

Uncle Henrik's house, she fell. She thought her ankle was

broken. Annemarie helped her up. Mrs. Johansen told Annemarie she was strong and brave. When they got to the steps of  the house, they stopped to rest. Annemarie noticed the package Peter had given Mr. Rosen in the grass by the steps. Mr. Rosen must have dropped the package on his way out the door. Annemarie asked what was in it. Mrs. Johansen would not tell her. She was worried their work was for nothing.

Annemarie offered to take the package to Uncle Henrik. So    Mrs. Johansen told Annemarie to get some food and put it     in a basket. Annemarie got cheese, an apple, and bread to    put in the basket. Her mother told her to hide the package    under the food. She told Annemarie to run very fast.

Annemarie was brave.

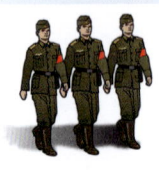

She told her that soldiers might stop her. If they did,

Annemarie was to say she was bringing lunch to her uncle,    who forgot his at home. It was cold outside as Annemarie ran down the path to the boat. The path was dark. It was hard    for her to run while carrying the basket. She heard a noise   and stopped. Nothing was there. Soon Annemarie came to a   place where the path split. The first path was wider but there might be soldiers on it. Annemarie stayed on the path that went through the woods. Now she knew why the people who   went to Uncle Henrik's boat needed guides. Annemarie kept    running. One more turn, and she would be on the path she   knew. Then, she heard another noise. She stopped and listened. She saw the last turn on the path but heard a growl. Four 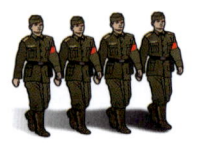   soldiers came around the turn with two dogs and stopped her.

Annemarie was brave.

CHAPTER 8

The Important Package

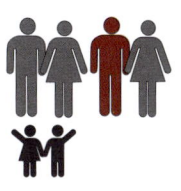

Annemarie remembered what her mother told her. She pretended she was taking lunch to her uncle, who left it at home. One   soldier asked her what she was doing. Annemarie held up her    basket. She said her uncle forgot his lunch and she was taking it to him. The dogs growled at the basket. The soldier asked why her uncle did not eat fish like other fishermen. Annemarie giggled and said her uncle did not like raw fish.

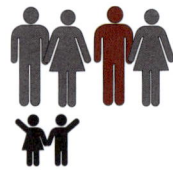

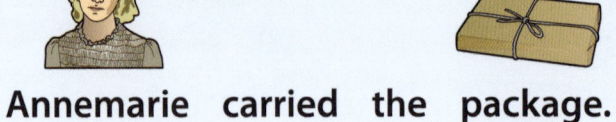

Annemarie carried the package.

The soldier took the bread out of the basket and gave it to    the dogs. He asked Annemarie whether she had seen anyone    else in the woods. Annemarie said she had not seen anyone.    The soldier kept digging in the basket. Annemarie hoped he would not find the package. Then he saw it. He demanded to   know what it was. Annemarie did not know what to do. She   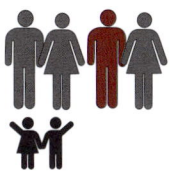  began to cry and said her mother and uncle would be angry    with her. She said she did not know what was in the package.  That was the truth.

Annemarie carried the package.

Then the soldiers tore the package open, but it was just a

handkerchief. He told her to stop crying. He threw the package to the ground. The dogs sniffed it but left it alone. The 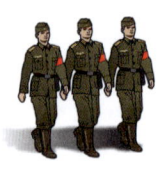    soldiers left. Annemarie picked up the package and ran to the boat. Uncle Henrik's boat was still there. Annemarie called out. When he saw her, he was worried. She told him she had his  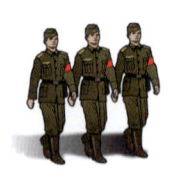  lunch. She said the soldiers had stopped her, and had taken     the bread. Uncle Henrik thanked Annemarie. She looked at the boat but did not see anyone. She did not know where   they were. Uncle Henrik told Annemarie that now everything 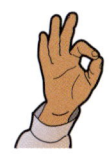   would be all right because she brought the package. He told    her to go home and tell her mother he would be home  in the evening.

Annemarie carried the package.

CHAPTER 9

The Handkerchief Saves People

After Annemarie returned from the boat, she went to the     hospital with her mother and Kirsti to get Mother's ankle taken care of. Later that night, Uncle Henrik returned. Uncle Henrik, Mrs. Johansen, Annemarie, and Kirsti ate dinner together. They talked while they ate dinner. Uncle Henrik said Annemarie had

to milk Blossom because no one else could do it. They all    laughed about that. Uncle Henrik offered to show Annemarie     the right way to milk a cow. So Annemarie and Uncle Henrik 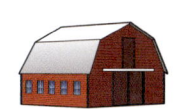    went to the barn to milk Blossom. Annemarie was confused and asked where the Rosens were on the boat. She hadn't seen   them. Uncle Henrik said they were there but hidden well. He   told Annemarie he would tell her a secret because she had

been so brave. Annemarie said she was scared, not brave. She said she didn't think about the danger. Uncle Henrik told her that was what being brave meant. He said Annemarie was brave because she did not think about the danger. He told Annemarie that he and other fishermen had hiding places in their boats.

A handkerchief saved people.

Uncle Henrik said people like Peter brought others to the boats.

Annemarie said she did not hear any people in the boat. She    asked Uncle Henrik if they heard her. Uncle Henrik said they could hear her and also the soldiers who searched the boat.    Annemarie asked why the handkerchief was important. Uncle   Henrik said it had something on it to confuse the dogs and    make it hard to smell people on the boat. He said Annemarie   came with the handkerchief just in time.

A handkerchief saved people.

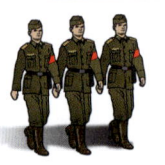

Right after she brought the package, German soldiers arrived with dogs. The handkerchief kept the dogs from smelling the   people. The Rosens and other passengers were taken safely to Sweden. Annemarie felt sad and asked Uncle Henrik if she   would ever see Ellen again. He said she would because the    war would end one day.

A handkerchief saved people.

CHAPTER 10

Ellen's Necklace

The war ended two years later, when Annemarie was 12. The   Johansens watched the celebration from the window of their     apartment. In the streets, people waved the flag of Denmark.  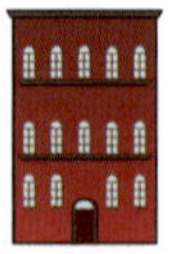 Annemarie thought about all of the empty apartments where    Jewish families lived. She hoped they would come back soon.

Mrs. Johansen took care of the Rosens' home while they were     in Sweden. Peter Neilson died helping the Jews escape.

Annemarie wore Ellen's necklace.

Before he died, Peter wrote a letter to the Johansens. He said he was proud and not afraid. When Annemarie went to visit     Peter's grave with her parents, they told her how Lise died.  Lise had also tried to help Jews escape. She was a hero.

Unit Three • Number the Stars • Chapter 10

Annemarie thought about her older sister. She went into her    bedroom and opened the trunk with Lise's things. From a skirt pocket, Annemarie pulled out Ellen's Star of David necklace.    She asked Mr. Johansen if he could fix the chain broken by accident.

Annemarie wore Ellen's necklace.

He said he could and she could give it to Ellen when Ellen

came back. Annemarie said she would wear it

until Ellen returned.

Annemarie wore Ellen's necklace.

The Diary of Anne Frank

Based on the book *The Diary of Anne Frank,* by Anne Frank.

Characters

Miep Gies	 Anne Frank

Mr. Frank	 Mrs. Frank	 Margot Frank
 Mrs. Van Daan	 Mr. Van Daan	 Peter Van Daan

Mr. Kraler	 Narrator

Act 1: Scene 1

Narrator

The scene remains the same throughout the play.

The scene is the top floor of a warehouse office building in Amsterdam, Holland. The upstairs space is exposed to the audience. The attic can also be seen. There is a large room in the center and two small rooms to each side. There are only a few pieces of furniture. The windows are painted over (this is called blacking out). It is a hiding place. There is only one way in or out. At the top of a staircase that leads to the room, the entrance is disguised as a bookcase.

The curtain rises on an empty stage. It is late afternoon, November, 1945. The door at the foot of the small stairwell opens. Mr. Frank walks up the stairs in full view of the audience. He is gentle-looking and European, with a trace of a German accent. Mr. Frank is about 42 years old. He looks very tired and sick. His clothes are old and worn.

Mr. Frank opens the door to one of the small rooms. He then closes it quickly. He looks around the room and sees a colorful scarf. He puts it around his neck and turns to leave. Mr. Frank notices a woman's white glove and picks it up. He breaks out crying. His self-control is gone.

We hear footsteps coming up the stairs. Miep Gies is coming to the room looking for Mr. Frank. Miep is a Dutch girl about 22 years old. She has her coat on and is ready to go home. Miep is pregnant. She is protective and compassionate toward Mr. Frank.

Miep		Are you all right, Mr. Frank?
Mr. Frank		Yes, Miep, yes.
Miep		It is late. Don't stay up here, Mr. Frank. There is no use in torturing yourself.
Mr. Frank		I have come to say good-bye. I am leaving here, Miep.
Miep		What do you mean? Where will you go? Amsterdam is your home! Your business is here. Now that the war is over, you are needed here.
Mr. Frank		There are too many memories here. I cannot stay. Everything reminds me of the past. You were so good to us. You took so many chances. I will always be thankful.
Miep		Wait, Mr. Frank. There are some papers here. We found them in a pile on the floor.
Mr. Frank		Burn all of them. I have no use for any of them.

Narrator		But, Mr. Frank stops to look at the papers. The paper on top says "Anne's diary. Monday, the 6th of July, 1942." He begins to read them.
Mr. Frank		Dear Diary, Since you and I are going to be great friends, I will start by telling you something about myself. My name is Anne Frank. I am 13 years old. I was born in Germany the 12th of June, 1929. My family is Jewish. We immigrated to Holland when Hitler came to power in Germany.
Anne **Mr. Frank**		[*Anne and Father say together*] My father was very successful. Things went very well for us until 1940. The war came. Hitler took over Holland. Then things got bad for the Jews.
Anne		There were so many rules. They forced Father to close his business. We had to sew yellow stars on our coats and wear them all the time. I had to turn my bike in. I couldn't go to Dutch school anymore. I couldn't go to the movies. I couldn't ride in an automobile or even on a street car. We children still had fun. Yesterday, Father told us we were going into hiding. We woke up at 5:00 this morning. We went to the space above Father's business. Three other people are joining us, the Van Daans, and their son, Peter. Father knew the Van Daans but we had never met them.

Intermission

Act 1: Scene 2

Narrator

It is early morning, July, 1942. The rooms are bare. They are clean and orderly.

Mr. Van Daan is a tall man in his late 40s. He is in the main room pacing back and forth. He is nervously smoking a cigarette. Mr. Van Daan is wearing expensive clothes and an overcoat.

Mrs. Van Daan is sitting on the couch in the big room. She is a pretty woman in her early 40s. She wears a fur coat over her other clothes.

Peter Van Daan is in a small room off the big room. He is 16 and shy and awkward. There is a black case at his feet. It is a carrier for his cat. The yellow Star of David is visible on his shirt.

Mrs. Van Daan

They are late. Something has happened to them! I know it!

Mr. Van Daan

They have two miles to walk. You can't expect . . . [*Trails off*]

Narrator

Mr. Frank comes up the stairs.

Mr. Frank

There are too many Green Police on the streets . . . we had to take the long way around.

Narrator		Margot Frank and Mrs. Frank come up the steps. Behind them are Miep and Mr. Kraler. They are all carrying bags and packages. Everyone in the Frank family is wearing the Star of David. It can be easily seen.
		Margot is 18. She is beautiful and shy. Mrs. Frank is a young mother. She is well-bred and reserved. She has a faint German accent.
		Mr. Kaler is Dutch. He is dependable and kind.
		Mr. Kaler and Miep go upstairs. They put the packages away.
		Mrs. Frank calls for her younger daughter.
Mrs. Frank		Anne?
Narrator		Anne comes running up the stairs. She is 13 and curious about everything. She is full of life. Anne is wearing a long, caped wool coat. She is carrying a school bag.
		Mr. Frank introduces everyone. Miep and Mr. Kraler are organizing their belongings.
Mr. Frank		We will have plenty of time to arrange things.
Miep		We put everything away. There is food in the cupboards. I must hurry. I have to go to the other side of town. I have to get ration books for you.

Mrs. Van Daan		Ration books? If they see our names on ration books, they will know we are here.
Miep		Don't worry. Your names will not be on them. I will be back later.
Mr. Frank		Thank you, Miep.
Mrs. Frank		We don't want to do anything illegal. We have always been honest.
Mr. Frank		But living here is against regulations.
Mr. Kraler		This is not the black market, Mrs. Frank. This is called the white market. Hundreds and hundreds of people are hiding in Amsterdam. There are people that want to help.
Narrator		The church bell rings. It's 8:00 a.m.
Mr. Kraler		I must go. I must be in my office by the time the workmen get here. Miep or I will come up each day. We will bring you food and news. We will take care of you. Tomorrow, I will bring a better bolt for the door. You should be the only ones who can open the door at the bottom of the stairs. We will make a code. [*He turns to Mr. Frank*] Oh. You will tell them about the noise?

Mr. Frank		I'll tell them.
Mr. Kraler		I never thought I would see the day when a man like you, Mr. Frank, has to go into hiding.
Narrator		Mr. Kraler runs to his business downstairs.
Mr. Frank		While the men are in the building below, we must have complete quiet. Every sound we make can be heard downstairs. The men come in about 8:30 a.m. and leave at 5:30 p.m. So, to be safe, between 8:00 and 6:00, we must only move when absolutely necessary.
Narrator		Mr. Frank stops. He hears the sound of marching feet in the street below them. Everyone is very still. They are paralyzed with fear. There is a window in the room to the right. Mr. Frank looks through it to the street below. Anne chases after him to see too. The soldiers pass without stopping. Everybody is relieved.
Mr. Frank		We must not wear shoes all day. We must only whisper. We must not run any water. We cannot use the sink or even the wash closet. We must burn everything we use. We cannot have any trash. This is the way we will live until the war is over. We have to survive.

Mrs. Frank This is how we will live until it is over.

Mr. Frank After 6:00 we can move around. We can talk and laugh. We can have supper. We can read, laugh, and play games. We can act like we are at home. And now we should go to our rooms. We need to be settled before 8:30 a.m. Mr. and Mrs. Van Daan, you will be upstairs. I am sorry but there is no room for Peter upstairs. He will be near us. This will be our common room. We will meet here to talk. We will eat and read in here. We will act like one big family. Mrs. Frank and I will sleep here.

When You Turn Out the Light

By Shel Silverstein and an Unknown Author

Based on the poem "No Difference," by Shel Silverstein and an Unknown Author.

Small as a peanut,

Big as a giant,

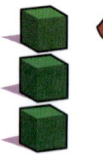

We're all the same size

When we "click, click" off the light.

Rich as a sultan,

Poor as a mite,

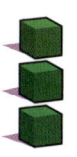

We're all worth the same

When we "click, click" off the light.

Red, black, or orange

Yellow or white,

We all look the same

When we "click, click" off the light.

So maybe the way

To make everything right

Is for you to just reach out

And "click, click" off the light!

UNIT FOUR
Global Awareness

Dragonwings

By Laurence Yep

Based on the book *Dragonwings,* by Laurence Yep.

CHAPTER

1	Land of the Demons	91
2	The Company	97
3	The Dragon Man	103
4	Tests	108
5	Windrider's Claws	113
6	The Demoness	118
7	Education	123
8	Earth, Wind, and Water	128
9	The Dragon Wakes	133
10	Life Changed	139
11	Exile	144
12	Dragonwings	150

CHAPTER 1

Land of the Demons

February to March 1903

Ever since I could remember, I had wanted to know about the    land of the Golden Mountain. My mother would never tell me    about it. Before I was born, my father left our home to go  there. He worked for the white demons. There was a lot of money to be made in the demon land, but it was

very dangerous.

Father lived in the land of the Golden Mountain.

Mother said she was too busy to answer my questions.

She and my grandmother were in charge of working our

small farm. When I talked about the Golden Mountain, Mother

would change the subject. She did not want to talk about

the Golden Mountain.

Father lived in the land of the Golden Mountain.

Mother made sure I knew one important thing about my father.  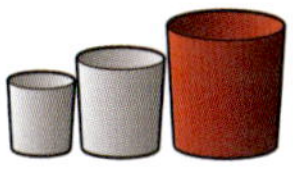 He made the most marvelous kites. As soon as I was big    enough to hold the string, Mother taught me how to fly a    kite. Father had made a special kite when he knew my mother    was pregnant. Mother said I could only fly it when I was

older and wiser—when I turned eight. I really wanted to fly my father's kite. When I turned eight, I felt I was old enough to get answers about the Golden Mountain. Grandmother decided to tell me about it. She said, "We call America the land of the Golden Mountain. There's a big mountain there full of gold.  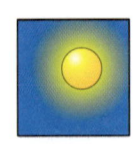   Men wait until the sun warms the mountain and then scoop     the gold into buckets. The white demons roam the mountain

and beat up any other men who try to get the gold.

Father is in a dangerous place."

Father lived in the land of the Golden Mountain.

I didn't know that I would find out first-hand about the     mountain. One day, my cousin Hand Clap returned from America. He brought a letter from Father. Father said it was time for me to be with him. Mother did not want me to go, but finally, she  agreed. When I first  saw my  father, I ran into his  arms. Father  smiled and said,  "Hello, boy. I've  waited a long  time to do this. Too long."

Father lived in the land of the  Golden Mountain.

CHAPTER 2

The Company

April 1903

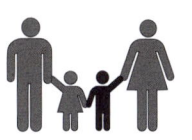

"So this is your boy," Uncle Bright Star said. "Yes, Uncle." Father pushed me toward him. Uncle stared at me and I stared back.    Uncle said, "Don't you know it's impolite to stare?" Then I said, "Then why are you doing it, sir?" My uncle said that I had character. Everyone laughed. I had been accepted.

Moon Shadow learned about the land of the Golden Mountain.

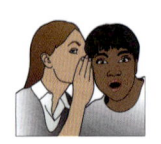

I asked, "Which one's the Golden Mountain?" Father said, "We haven't seen the Golden Mountain. Maybe we'll come across the mountain yet." Father whispered to me, "Stick close to me, Moon Shadow, and don't be afraid. There are a lot of demons here." We set off to Chinatown. That is where the Tang

(Chinese) people live in America.

Moon Shadow learned about the land of the Golden Mountain.

There were no women on the streets, only men. We stepped into a small, neat, three-story building painted bright red and green. We went upstairs. It was used as a kitchen and resting room. Our sleeping quarters were on the third floor. The dinner that night was the best I had ever had. First, Uncle toasted me. Then, he toasted the Company. They all worked for the

Company. Next, they brought out a new set of clothes and a

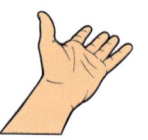

hat for me to wear. Father said, "They've given you something

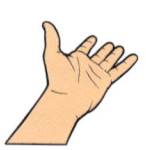

for your body, but I am giving you something for your soul."

He went upstairs and came back with the most marvelous kite

I had seen. It was painted in bright colors and was shaped

like a butterfly.

Moon Shadow learned about the land of the Golden Mountain.

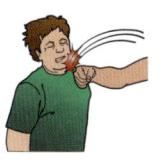

At that moment, the doorbell rang. It was Black Dog. He told us the white demons were drunk and ready to beat up the    Tang people. Then, we heard windows shattering, and yelling    from the demons. We waited silently for the demons to go   away. Once we knew they had gone, we began boarding up    the windows. Black Dog laughed, "Welcome to the land of the demons, boy."

Moon Shadow learned about the land of the Golden Mountain.

CHAPTER 3

The Dragon Man

April 1903

As Father led me to my room, I wondered about his name,

Windrider. I asked, "Father, why do they call you Windrider?"

Then, he told me a story.

Windrider told Moon Shadow a story.

Father said, "One night, I went to sleep. When I woke up

I was on a beach. I saw the Dragon King lying there on

the beach. The Dragon King said I used to be a dragon!

When I was a dragon, I was the greatest doctor of all dragons.

He said I was a show-off when it came to flying."

Windrider told Moon Shadow a story.

Then Father said, "Dragon King was hurt. He asked me to

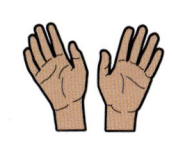

heal him. Without thinking, my hands knew what to do.

He asked, 'How can I ever reward you?' I asked him to

make me a dragon again. He could not do that. So, he

made some shiny wings. His soldiers pasted the wings to my

back. I felt them tug at my back. Then I spread my wings

and saw how beautiful they were!"

Windrider told Moon Shadow a story.

Father said, "It would take all night to describe the dragon kingdom. I still remember the Dragon King's throne. It was    made of gold. Like a mirror, you could see anything in it.    Then, the Dragon King asked me what I wanted to see.     I told him I wanted to see my wife. I saw your mother   singing a lullaby to you. Finally, it was time for me to return to my living world."

Father sat quietly. Then, he said, "The others say it was just a dream. The only proof I have is a sore back and ribs." I said, "I believe you were there Father. Something as beautiful as that has to be true." Then, there was a knock at my bedroom door.   It was my uncle. He gave me a little toy he had made. It   was a carving of a monkey. I held it close as I fell to sleep.

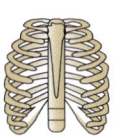

Windrider told Moon Shadow a story.

CHAPTER 4

Tests

April 1903 to February 1904

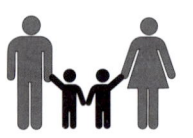

Over the next year, I learned that the Company was more than a group of men. We were brothers banded together. I was    treated like a man, not like a boy. Father spoke the language of the white demons best. (Some of the Chinese people in town called white men demons. This is a name for

mean people.) Father was often sent into town to pick

up dirty laundry. Then, he would deliver the clean laundry.

Father had many skills.

One day we met a demon. This demon was big and cheerful.

He was driving a horseless carriage (a car) that had broken

down. A long time ago, people called cars "horseless carriages."

He asked Father, "Do you know anything about a     horseless carriage?" Father had never fixed a horseless carriage in his whole life, but he looked into the engine anyway.

And he fixed it!

Father had many skills.

The demon was very happy with Father's work. He offered us    money, but Father would not accept it. So, he reached into his pocket and gave Father a business card. It said, "Oliver Alger,

Real Estate Agent. Properties sold and managed. 1200 Polk St."

I asked Father how he knew what to do. He said he just let

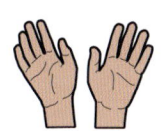

his hands do the work. I asked, "Do you think that was the

Dragon King? Do you think it was a test?" Father stared at

me and said, "You talk too much."

Father had many skills.

When we got home, Father showed me a newspaper called  the New York Herald. It said that two demon men, the    Wright brothers, had flown an airplane. Some of the men told Father to build a flying machine, too. Then, he would be able to fly Mother to join us in the land of the Golden Mountain.

Father had many skills.

CHAPTER 5

Windrider's Claws

February 1904 to May 1905

Black Dog got into  trouble with the white  demons. He owed them  money for 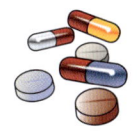 drugs so they  shot him. His  friends carried him to the  Company and put him to  bed. They  discussed how to  help him pay the  money back. They also  said the  demons often tried to trap the Tang by selling drugs to them.

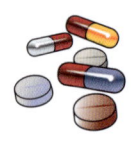

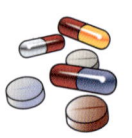

Black Dog promised to stop taking drugs.

Father and Moon Shadow had hard times.

It was not long before Black Dog was back to stealing money 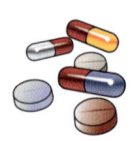   and buying drugs. One day he took me to town to pick up    dirty laundry. I carried the money bag. He hit me over the    head, stole the money, and then ran away.

Father and Moon Shadow had hard times.

Father went out looking for Black Dog. He was being protected by a group of men called The Sleepers. When Father found  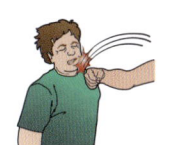  Black Dog, he beat him up. A man in the group pulled a    gun on me. Then, my father accidentally killed him. The others told Father he should leave town until everything settled down.

Father and Moon Shadow had hard times.

Father and I  left the 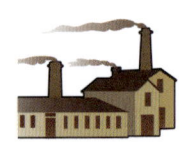 Company the next  day. Father told them he was going to work for a  demon, Mister Alger.  He said we would stay with  demons, who rent  houses to  people for  money. They are called  landlords. The  Company thought we were 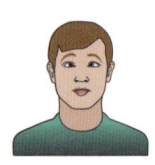 crazy for wanting to live among the  demons. At the  farewell  party, everyone brought  gifts. Uncle gave us a porcelain  cup with  soil and  incense in it. Incense is a special  stick that is  burned when people 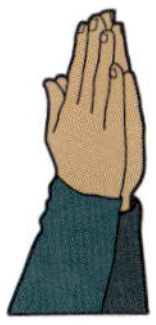 pray. The  soil was from  Uncle's last trip back to  China. Uncle told us to  burn the  incense for  protection. Father said, "We'll give it a special place. It will  help us pray for  safety."

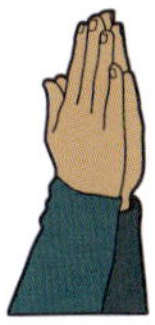

Father and  Moon Shadow had hard times.

CHAPTER 6

The Demoness

May 1905

Father said we would make lots of money in our new place.

We would fix machines for the demons. We would live in the

stable behind our landlady's house. We would sleep on mats

and blankets there. At our new place, all of the houses on

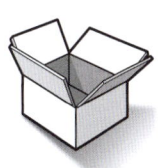

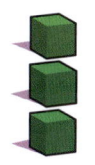

the street looked like square boxes. They were all the same   except for one, our landlady's house. It was a large Victorian home with eight sides. Father said, "It's time for us to meet our landlady."

Windrider and Moon Shadow had a new home.

This was the first lady demon, a demoness, I saw up close.    Her name was Miss Whitlaw. She was tiny and polite. She smiled at us. She had a friendly twinkle in her eye. She    invited us in. Miss Whitlaw gave me milk and gingerbread    cookies. They were the best cookies I had ever tasted.

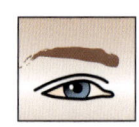

Windrider and Moon Shadow had a new home.

Robin was Miss Whitlaw's niece. She invited me to look through her picture viewer. It was like a small camera you look through. They used it for looking at pictures. I could not believe my eyes. Robin said, "That's Niagara Falls. The picture viewer lets us travel all around the world without even leaving the house."

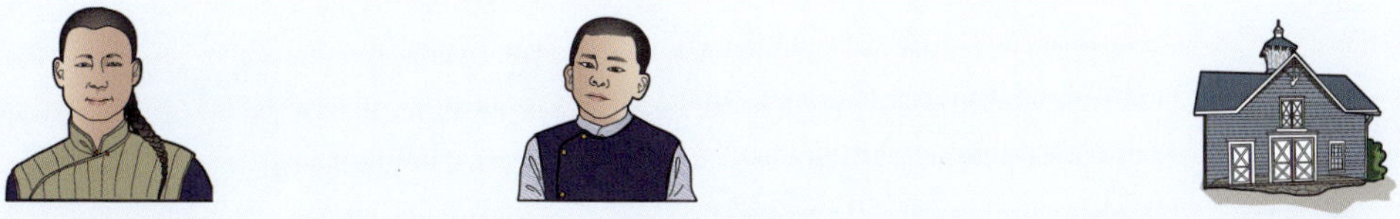

Windrider and Moon Shadow had a new home.

Next, Robin showed me their stained-glass window. A stained-glass window is made of colored glass. It was tall and rectangular. In the center was a great dragon, breathing yellow and red flames. Robin said dragons were wicked animals that eat people and destroy towns. I looked at Father. I was confused. Father looked at me and shook his head. I felt sad that Miss Whitlaw and Robin did not know that dragons of the sea were wise  and kind.

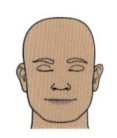

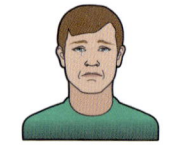

Windrider and Moon Shadow had a new home.

CHAPTER 7

Education

May to June 1905

Each day, while Father was at work, he allowed me to have   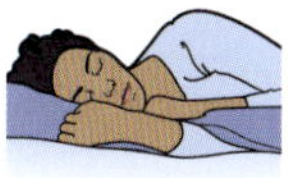 30 minutes of free time. I could use this time to nap, play, or read. I decided to teach Miss Whitlaw and Robin about dragons. They decided to teach me how to read and write in English.

Moon Shadow was a student and a teacher.

I told Miss Whitlaw about my father's dream of building    an airplane. I asked her to help me write a letter to the    Wright brothers. Miss Whitlaw was my writing teacher. I was    her student. I wanted to help my father learn about airplanes. I was his teacher!

Moon Shadow was a student and a teacher.

This was my  letter:

> To the Honorable Wrights:
>
> This is to inform you that I am a boy of eleven. I have greatly admired your feats of daring. My father wants to fly too. Can you help him? We need to know how to shape the propellers and wings. Father says that no one else in the world knows as much as you do about airplanes. Thank you.

2

Two weeks later, I received a  letter from the  Wrights'  Bicycle Shop. This was their  letter:

> Dear Mr. Lee,
>
> My brother and I are always happy to meet another flying enthusiast. Our brotherhood is too small to lose any one of us. Enclosed you will find some tables and diagrams that should prove of some service to you. If we can be of any further assistance to you, please let us know.

I waited anxiously for Father to come home. When he    arrived, I read the letter to him. He was angry that I told     Miss Whitlaw about his dream of flying. He crumpled up the    letter and threw it in the corner. The next morning, Father    picked up the letter and smoothed it out. He looked at the     tables and diagrams. Then he said, "Can you help me write  another letter to them?" I said, "I can try."

Moon Shadow was a student and a teacher.

CHAPTER 8

Earth, Wind, and Water

June to September 1905

We wrote many letters to the Wright brothers. They answered    Father's questions right away. Their instructions helped Father make bigger glider kites. The big gliders were small models   of the real airplanes. One Saturday morning, Father invited

Miss Whitlaw and Robin for a picnic. After the picnic, we took turns flying Father's newest kite. Father's turn was last. I watched him closely. He pulled a paper from his pocket and tied it to the end of the kite. Next, he pulled out his pocketknife and cut the string. He wanted to see how far it would fly on its own. We were all disappointed because it didn't go very far.    Father promised to make us new kites.

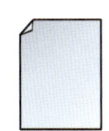

Moon Shadow learned from many people.

The next Saturday, Father had to work. Robin invited me to fly her new kite. I was afraid. I could hear demon boys playing    in the streets, but Robin told me that the biggest boy, Jack, was afraid of the sight of his own blood. When we walked   outside, Jack stopped playing. He began making fun of me   by saying, "Ching Chong, Chinaman." I looked at him and said,

"I no like that song. I think it stupid." Then he said,   "You think I'm stupid?" Jack ran toward me. He expected  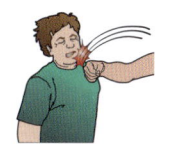 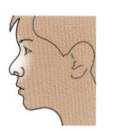 me to run away. Instead, I punched him in the nose.

Moon Shadow learned from many people.

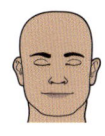

Jack sat on the sidewalk with blood running down his face.   Suddenly I realized that demon boys were like the Tang boys  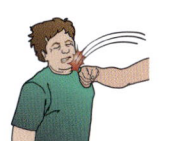   I knew at home. You had to punch the biggest and toughest one to be accepted. From that day on, we all became friends.

Moon Shadow learned from many people.

CHAPTER 9

The Dragon Wakes

December 1905 to April 1906

Winter came and we were not yet  rich, but we were doing very well. We saved our  money. We  hoped to  open our own  repair shop in  San Francisco. However, I  started to have a  terrible feeling that something  bad was about to happen.

I was right. Early one morning after I had dressed, I went   outside to pump water. The morning was filled with soft,    dreamy colors. Just then, I felt a rumble in the ground.   An earthquake! I didn't believe it at first, but buildings began falling down all around me. It felt like the whole world was coming unglued.

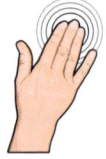

San Francisco had an earthquake.

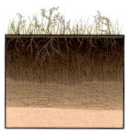

Most of the houses on Polk Street fell to the ground.    Miss Whitlaw's house was the only house standing. Father    and I ran inside to check on Miss Whitlaw and Robin. They    were safe. Miss Whitlaw said we must help save those who    were crushed under the rubble. We could hear people calling   for help. We knew we could not do it alone. Miss Whitlaw  said, "We'll get help from the others."

San Francisco had an earthquake.

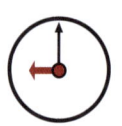

Little by little we cleared piles of rubble. We saved as many demons as we could. After several hours of work, Father said, "I have not heard anyone calling in the last hour. The people still under the rubble are not alive." Miss Whitlaw agreed. We all went back to Miss Whitlaw's house for food and water.

Sadly, the water pump was dry.

San Francisco had an earthquake.

The earthquake caused fires. One started burning south of Polk Street, and it was moving toward us. Another one started burning on the other side of us. About four hours later an army of    demon soldiers arrived to rescue us. They told us about all the fires. They told us to gather our belongings, and they would take us to Golden Gate Park. We helped Miss Whitlaw gather

her things. She packed the  picture viewer and the  stained-glass  dragon window.  Miss Whitlaw suggested we  check on our  people at the  Company. As  Miss Whitlaw and Robin  drove away, she  said, "We'll  meet you in the  park." Father said, "See  you there."

San Francisco had an earthquake.

CHAPTER 10

Life Changed

April to May 1906

Uncle brought the wagon to pick us up. Uncle took us to the   Golden Gate Park. On the way to the park, we passed many    white people. They looked shocked. They could not believe this happened to them. Yesterday, money was important to them.

Today, only food and water were important.

In San Francisco, life had changed.

We found Miss Whitlaw and Robin at the park. However, the    Tang people were placed in separate tents from Americans.     When our tent became flooded with water, Miss Whitlaw invited us to stay with her.

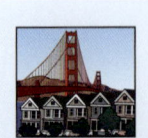

In San Francisco, life had changed.

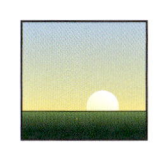

The next morning, a young officer entered her tent. He told   us, "Come along, you two. We're moving you out." Miss Whitlaw argued with the officer, but he said we must leave. The officers found all of the Tang people in camp. They marched us all   out of the camp. We were not sure where they were taking   us but, for sure, it was out of San Francisco. Uncle decided to take charge. He said some American businesses could not make money without the Tang people. They paid us very little money. They will have to pay white people more money to do 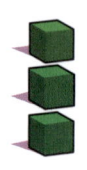  the same work. This will leave less money for them and their businesses. Most of the business people agreed we should stay.

In San Francisco, life had changed.

We went back to Chinatown to rebuild the Company. The     Company days were filled with joy and laughter. Father helped the Company, but he still had flying on his mind. He said we should not give up on our dream of flying. Uncle laughed and said that Father made no sense. Eventually, Father and I left the Company to make our dreams come true.

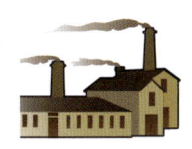

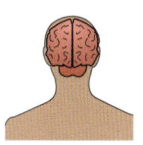

In San Francisco, life had changed.

CHAPTER 11

Exile

May 1906 to September 1909

Father and I moved to the foothills above Oakland. We    borrowed Miss Whitlaw's wagon for the move. We lived in an 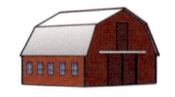  old barn. It was next to a beautiful mansion that was ruined in the earthquake. The view from the hills was amazing. At night, thousands of lights glittered like gold. At last, I found the Golden Mountain. But it was not made of gold nuggets.   It was made of people like the Whitlaws and the Company.

Father and Moon Shadow followed their dreams.

One day, we received a letter from Mother and Grandmother.    Mother said how proud she was that Father had followed his    dreams of flying. She said I should continue to support and love Father. I knew she was blushing with pride.

Father and Moon Shadow followed their dreams.

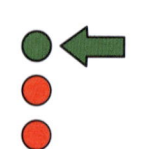

3 It took three years to build the flying machine. Father and  I named it Dragonwings. By the end of summer, we were  ready to fly it. We would take Dragonwings to the top of the hill. Father would use the money we saved to hire a team of horses to pull the wagon to the top. I was proud that Father wanted to be a dragon again. But the next day,

Black Dog came to our house. He looked through our things to

find money to steal. When I tried to stop Black Dog, he held

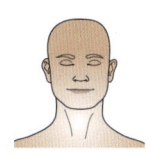

a knife to my throat. Just then, Father walked in and yelled,

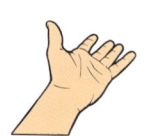

"Don't harm him." Black Dog said, "Give me your money. How

important is that flying machine? Is it more important than your

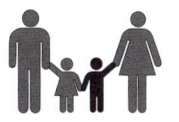

son's life? Give me all your money!" Father gave Black Dog all the money he had saved. His dreams were not as important  as his son.

Father and Moon Shadow followed their dreams.

Now, we didn't have any money to pay the rent. The landlord    got mad at Father. He gave us three days to get money to   pay the rent. We knew that would be impossible. We knew we  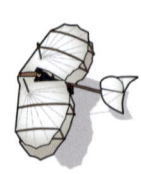 had to leave. We could not take Dragonwings with us. We had no money to pay for horses to haul the wagon. "Maybe this   is the final test in life," I said. Father thought for a bit and laughed, "Yes, maybe it is."

Father and Moon Shadow followed their dreams.

CHAPTER 12

Dragonwings

September 1909 to June 1910

It was way past sunrise when I woke up. Father was still    rolled up in his blanket. We heard a knock at the barn door,  and there stood Hand Clap. It was as if he had appeared   by magic. He called over his shoulder, "Hey, everybody, they're here." I heard the clink of a harness and the rattle of an old wagon. The men from the Company were following close behind.

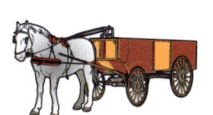

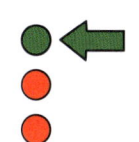

"We're here to help you get that flying machine to the top of that hill," Uncle said.

Father and Moon Shadow were helped by family and friends.

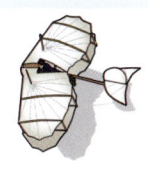

We put Dragonwings on the wagon. For the first time,   Dragonwings emerged into the world. "We'll go to the very

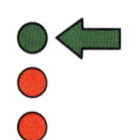

top. That's where the wind is best," said Father. When we were almost to the top of the hill, we saw two figures stomping up the hill. Miss Whitlaw's face lit up when she saw us. "Thank goodness," Robin puffed, "I thought we might be late." Robin and I took our places to help get Dragonwings off the ground. Father laid belly down on the flying machine. Dragonwings    lurched forward and took off. Everyone cheered. Father was

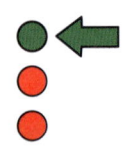

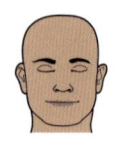

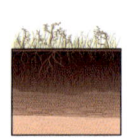

really flying. About five minutes later, the wind began to blow harder. I held my breath. Dragonwings rose into the air. Then it headed down the hillside toward the bay. It crashed into the hillside. We rushed to check on Father. He was alive, but his leg and two ribs were broken. I felt sad.

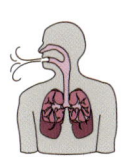

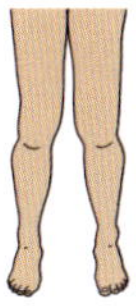

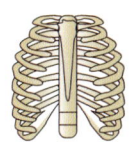

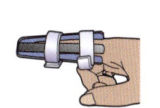

Father and Moon Shadow were helped by family and friends.

Father awoke the next day. He said, "I'm not going to build

another flying machine. When I was up there, I wanted you   and your mother with me. I know now that my family means    more to me than flying." Uncle said, "Maybe that crash knocked some sense into you." Hand Clap and Uncle assured Father that he was still considered a partner in the Company. Father said, "But I don't even have a dollar to my name." "I'll lend you     the money," Uncle said. Father agreed. Hand Clap and Uncle said they were getting too old to run the Company. They said

Father and I would be the perfect team to take over.

Father and Moon Shadow were helped by family and friends.

Father and I moved back into the Company's new building. It

took months for Father's bones to heal. During that time, we

never lost touch with the Whitlaws. I would either call or visit

them every Sunday. In summer, Father was able to pay money

to the demon officials. Then he sailed to the Middle Kingdom to bring Mother back. I knew we would have many future 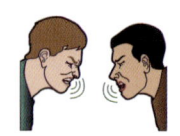  problems to solve, but I was not afraid of them. I knew that Mother and Father gave me courage. Father had the courage to follow his dreams. Mother had the courage to let us live in   America. We would be strong together.

Father and Moon Shadow were helped by family and friends.

Sadako and the Thousand Paper Cranes

By Eleanor Coerr

Based on the book *Sadako and the Thousand Paper Cranes,* by Eleanor Coerr.

Characters

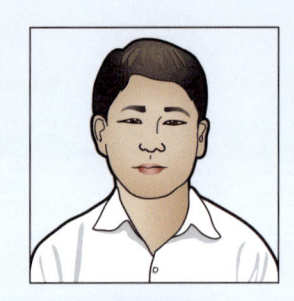

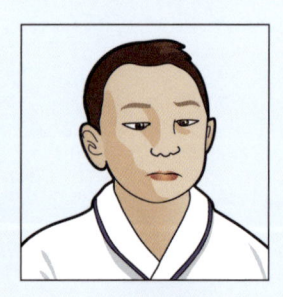

Sadako	Masahiro	Eiji
Narrator	Mrs. Sasaki	Mr. Sasaki
Chizuko	Teacher	Kenji
Nurse	Doctor	Mitsue

Act 1: Scene 1

Narrator		It's morning in a Japanese home, August 1954. Sadako Sasaki is a little girl from Hiroshima, Japan. She is just waking up, and is full of excitement. Sadako runs into the room where her sister and two brothers are still sleeping.
Sadako		Get up, lazybones! It's Peace Day!
Narrator		Masahiro, Sadako's 14-year-old brother, groans and yawns. Slowly, Mitsue, Sadako's 9-year-old sister, and Eiji, Sadako's 6-year-old brother, start to wake up too.
Eiji		Sadako, help me get dressed for Peace Day.
Sadako		Okay, get up and come here.
Narrator		After Sadako helps Eiji get dressed, she rushes like a whirlwind into the kitchen, where her mother is preparing bean soup and rice for breakfast.
Sadako		Oh, Mother! I can hardly wait to go to the carnival. Can we please hurry with breakfast?
Mrs. Sasaki		You are 11 years old and should know better! You must not call it a carnival. Every year on August 6th we remember those who died when the atom bomb was dropped on our city. It's a Memorial Day.

Narrator		Mr. Sasaki, Sadako's father, enters the kitchen from the back porch.
Mr. Sasaki		That is right, Sadako chan, you must show respect. Your own grandmother was killed that awful day.
Sadako		But I do respect Oba chan. I pray for her spirit every morning. It's just that I'm so happy today.
Mr. Sasaki		As a matter of fact, it's time for our prayers now.
Narrator		The Sasaki family gathers around a little altar shelf. Oba chan's picture is there in a gold frame. Sadako looks at the ceiling and wonders if her grandmother's spirit is floating somewhere above the altar.
Mr. Sasaki		Sadako chan! Pay attention to your prayers.
Narrator		Mr. Sasaki prays for the spirits of their ancestors, his barbershop, and his fine children. He also prays that his family will be protected from the atom bomb disease called leukemia. Many still die from the disease, even though the atom bomb had been dropped on Hiroshima 9 years before. The bomb had filled the air with radiation, a poison, that stays inside people for a long time. After the prayers, the Sasaki family eats breakfast and prepares to go to Peace Day.

Act 1: Scene 2

Narrator		The family arrives at the Peace Park and Sadako runs ahead to meet up with her best friend, Chizuko. Chizuko and Sadako enter the Peace Park to look at the walls of the memorial building. On the walls are photographs of the dead and dying in a ruined city. The atom bomb—they call it the Thunderbolt—had turned Hiroshima into a desert.
Sadako		I remember the Thunderbolt. There was the flash of a million suns. Then the heat prickled my eyes like needles.
Chizuko		How can you possibly remember anything? You were only a baby then.
Sadako		Well, I do!
Narrator		The day passes quickly. Sadako enjoys looking at all the things to buy and smelling the good food. The worst part is seeing people with ugly, whitish scars. The atom bomb had burned them so badly that they no longer looked human. If any of the bomb victims come near Sadako, she turns away quickly. Excitement grows as the sun goes down. Mr. Sasaki carefully lights candles inside six lanterns—one for each member of the family. The lanterns carry names of relatives who died because of the Thunderbolt.

Intermission

Act 1: Scene 3

Narrator		It's now the beginning of autumn. Sadako rushes home with the good news. She kicks off her shoes and throws open the door with a bang. Sadako's mother is in the kitchen.
Sadako		I'm home! The most wonderful thing has happened. Guess what!
Mrs. Sasaki		Many wonderful things happen to you Sadako chan. I can't even guess.
Sadako		The big race on Field Day! I have been chosen from the bamboo class to be on the relay team. Just think. If we win, I'll be sure to get on the team in junior high school next year!
Narrator		Sadako thinks of only one thing from then on—the race. She practices every day at school and runs all the way home too. At last, the big day arrives. All her family and friends are there. Sadako is nervous.
Mrs. Sasaki		Do your best, and don't worry. You will run as fast as you can.
Narrator		When it's her turn to run, she runs with all the strength she has. Sadako's heart is thumping painfully against her ribs, and she feels very dizzy. She hears cheering. Her family and friends run over to her.
Mrs. Sasaki		Sadako! You won! Your team won!

Narrator		Sadako continues to run all winter to improve her speed, but sometimes she feels dizzy after running. She decides not to tell her family. The dizziness doesn't go away. In fact, it gets worse. One morning when Sadako is running to school, everything seems to whirl around her and she sinks to the ground. A teacher rushes over to help.
Sadako		I . . . I guess I'm just tired.
Teacher		I'm going to tell your father, and we are going to the hospital.

Act 2: Scene 1

Narrator		At the hospital, Sadako is in an exam room where a nurse X-rays her chest and takes some of her blood. Four doctors come in to look at Sadako. One of them shakes his head and gently strokes her hair. Her family arrives at the hospital and talks with the doctors.
Mr. Sasaki		Leukemia! But that . . . that's impossible.
Narrator		Sadako hears her family talking with the doctors and can't understand. Of course she doesn't have leukemia. The atom bomb hasn't even scratched her. The family enters Sadako's room.
Mrs. Sasaki		You must stay here for a little while. But I'll come every evening, and after school, your brothers and sisters will come.

Sadako		Do I really have the atom bomb disease?
Mr. Sasaki		The doctors want to take some tests. That's all. They might keep you here for a few weeks. Is there anything you want?
Narrator		Sadako shakes her head. All she really wants is to go home. She is going to miss graduation and the new racing team. She tries not to cry.

Act 2: Scene 2

Narrator		It's the next day and Sadako wakes up hoping it's all a bad dream. She realizes it isn't when the nurse comes in to give her a shot. Now, in the afternoon, Chizuko comes to visit.
Chizuko		Shut your eyes. Now you can look.
Sadako		What is it?
Chizuko		I've figured out a way for you to get well. Watch!
Narrator		Chizuko cuts a piece of gold paper into a large square. In a short time, she folds it over and over into a beautiful crane. Sadako is confused.

Sadako		But how can that paper bird make me well?
Chizuko		Don't you remember that old story about the crane? It's supposed to live for 10,000 years. If a sick person folds 1,000 paper cranes, the gods will grant her wish and make her healthy again. Here is your first one.
Sadako		Thank you, Chizuko chan. I'll never part with it. Help me make one on my own!
Narrator		The girls make 10 together and line them up on the table.
Chizuko		Now you only have 990 left to make.
Narrator		It's now evening, and Masahiro, Sadako's brother, brings Sadako's homework from school. He looks over at the paper cranes.
Masahiro		There isn't enough room on that small table to show off your birds. I'll hang them from the ceiling for you.
Sadako		Do you promise to hang every crane I make?
Masahiro	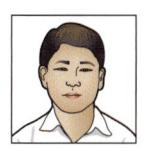	Yes.

Sadako		That's fine! Then you'll hang the whole 1,000?
Masahiro		1,000! You're joking!
Narrator		Sadako tells him the story of the cranes.
Masahiro		You tricked me! But I'll do it anyhow.

Act 2: Scene 3

Narrator		In the next few months, people keep bringing Sadako paper to make cranes. She becomes very good and very fast at making them. Sadako is feeling weaker and weaker. One day, when she is feeling very tired, the nurse wheels her onto the porch for some sunshine. There is a boy on the porch named Kenji. He is also in a wheelchair.
Sadako		Hello! I'm Sadako.
Kenji	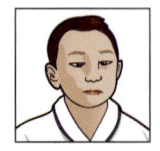	I'm Kenji. I've been in the hospital for a long time. My parents died. I used to live with my aunt. She's so old that she comes to see me only once a week. I read most of the time. It really doesn't matter because I'll die soon. I have leukemia from the bomb.

Sadako		But you can't have leukemia. You weren't even born then.
Kenji	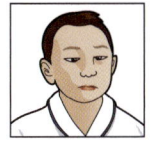	That isn't important. The poison was in my mother's body, and I got it from her.
Sadako		You can make paper cranes like I do, so that a miracle can happen.
Kenji		I know about the cranes, but it's too late. Even the gods can't help me now.
Nurse		Kenji, how do you know such things?
Kenji	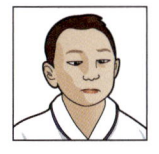	I just know. And besides, I can read my blood count on the chart. Every day it gets worse.
Nurse		What a talker! You are tiring yourself. It's time to go back inside.
Narrator		Sadako makes a big paper crane and sends it to Kenji's room.

Intermission

Act 2: Scene 4

Narrator		It's now a few days later. The nurse comes in to Sadako's room and tells her that Kenji has died. Sadako cries.
Nurse		Let's sit by the window and talk.
Sadako		Do you think Kenji is up there on a star island?
Nurse		Wherever he is, I'm sure he is happy now. He has shed that tired, sick body and his spirit is free.
Sadako		I'm going to die next, aren't I?
Nurse		Of course not! Come and let me see you fold another paper crane before you go to sleep. After you finish 1,000 birds, you'll live to be an old lady.

Act 2: Scene 5

Narrator		Time has gone on. Sadako is growing pale and has no energy. Sadako is not eating as much as she used to. Her parents and brother bring her all her favorite foods—an egg roll, chicken and rice, pickled plums, and bean cakes. Sadako tries to eat, but her mouth hurts too much and she can't chew.

Sadako		I'm such a turtle!
Mrs. Sasaki		It's all right. You'll be better soon. Maybe when the sun comes out.
Masahiro		Oh, I almost forgot! I have a present for you. Here, this is for another crane.
Narrator		Masahiro hands Sadako a crumpled up piece of paper.
Sadako		Mmmmm . . . It smells like candy. I hope the gods like chocolate.
Narrator		Everyone laughs. It feels good to laugh. Sadako smooths out the paper and makes another crane, number 541. As Mrs. Sasaki leaves the room, she whispers a poem to Sadako.
Mrs. Sasaki		O flock of heavenly cranes, Cover my child with your wings.

Act 3: Scene 1

Narrator		The weather is getting warmer. Sadako thinks she is feeling a little better.
Sadako		I'm over halfway to 1,000 cranes, so something good is going to happen.

Narrator		Sadako's appetite is coming back and her pain is going away. She is going home for a visit. She is so excited that she makes more cranes to keep the magic going . . . 622. All her friends come to visit her at home. By the end of the week, she is very tired and sits quietly.
Mr. Sasaki		Sadako certainly has good manners now. Oba chan's spirit must be pleased to see how ladylike her granddaughter has become.
Mrs. Sasaki		How can you say that! I would rather have our lively Sadako back.
Sadako		I'm making everyone sad.
Mr. Sasaki		There now, don't worry. After a good night's rest you'll feel fine.

Act 3: Scene 2

Narrator		It's now the next day. Sadako is back at the hospital. She is tired, and is drifting in and out of a strange half-sleep.
Sadako		When I die, will you put my favorite bean cakes on the altar for my spirit?
Mr. Sasaki		Hush! That will not happen for many, many years. Don't give up now, Sadako chan. You have to make only a few hundred more cranes.

Sadako		I **will** get better, and someday I'll race like the wind.
Narrator		Now Sadako is getting blood transfusions every day.
Doctor		I know it hurts, but we must keep on trying.
Narrator	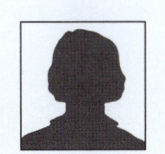	Sadako is in constant pain, and she is afraid of dying. The golden crane reminds her that there is always hope. Mrs. Sasaki spends more and more time at the hospital now. Her family brings her a special present, a silk kimono with cherry blossoms on it.
Sadako		Why did you do it? I'll never be able to wear it, and silk costs so much money.
Mr. Sasaki		Sadako chan, your mother stayed up late last night to finish sewing it. Try it on for her.
Narrator		Mrs. Sasaki helps Sadako out of bed and into the kimono. She looks like a princess. Her friends from school also come to visit her.
Chizuko		You look better in that outfit than in school clothes.
Sadako		Then I'll wear it to classes every day when I'm well again.

Narrator		Sadako is having a great visit with her family and friends. She is sitting stiffly in the chair and trying to ignore the pain. When her parents leave, they almost look cheerful to Sadako. Before she goes to sleep, Sadako manages to fold only one paper crane . . . 644. It's the last one she will make.

Act 3: Scene 3

Narrator		Sadako is growing weaker. She thinks more about death. She wants to forget about death, but it keeps creeping back into her mind. Today she sees her mother crying.
Sadako		Don't cry. Please don't cry.
Narrator		Sadako tries to make a paper crane, but she is too weak.
Sadako		I can't even make a crane. I've turned into a real turtle!
Doctor		It's time to rest. You can make more birds tomorrow.

Narrator

It's the next morning and Sadako is waking up. Her family is there visiting. Sadako smiles at them. They are part of a warm, loving circle. Nothing will ever change that. Sadako looks at the flock of paper cranes hanging by the window. The breeze makes them sway like they are flying.

Sadako sighs and closes her eyes. She never wakes up. Sadako Sasaki dies. It is October 25, 1955.

Her classmates fold 356 cranes so that 1,000 could be buried with her. In a way, she got her wish. In 1958, a statue of Sadako was built in Hiroshima Peace Park. It shows Sadako standing on top of a granite mountain of paradise holding a paper crane. People place thousands of paper cranes beneath her statue every August 6th, Peace Day. The engraving on the statue says:

This is our cry, this is our prayer.
Peace in the world.

One Tribe

Based on the song "One Tribe," by the Black Eyed Peas.

One tribe, one time, one planet, one race

It's all one blood, don't care about your face

Color of your eye or the tone of your skin

Don't care where ya are, don't care where ya been

We gonna go is where we wanna be

The place where the language is unity

The continent is called Pangaea

The main ideas are connected like a spear

There is no propaganda

Cause man I'm lovin this . . . peace!

There's . . .

One tribe y'all

We one tribe y'all

We are one people

Let's catch amnesia, forget about all that evil

We are one people

One tribe, one time, one planet, one

Race, one love, one people, one

too many things that's causing one

To forget about the main cause

Connecting, uniting

But the evil is seeded and alive in us

So our weapons are colliding

And our peace is sinking like Poseidon

But, we know that the one

The Evil One is threatened by the sum

So he will try and separate the sum

But he didn't know we had a way to overcome

We are rejuvenated by the beating of the drum

We will come together by the cipher of the hum

One love, one blood, one people

One heart, one beat, we are equal

We are connected like the Internet, united

Let love and peace lead you

Help each other make these changes

Brother sister rearrange this

way I'm thinkin that we can change this

bad condition wait . . .

Use you mind and not yo' greed

Let's connect and then proceed

This is something I believe

We are one we're all just people

Let's, let's catch amnesia, Lord help me out

Trying to figure out what it's all about

Cause we're one in the same

Same joy, same pain

We need to, be one

One world, one love, one passion

One tribe, one understanding

Cause you, and me, can be-come one